Hal•Leonard
INSTRUMENTAL
PLAY-ALONG

AUDIO
ACCESS
INCLUDED

CELLO

BEST OF METALLICA

T0066001

PLAYBACK+
Speed • Pitch • Balance • Loop

To access audio visit:
www.halleonard.com/mylibrary

1408-3905-0150-5660

Recorded by Scott Seelig

Cherry Lane Music Company
Educational Director/Project Supervisor: Susan Poliniak
Director of Publications: Mark Phillips
Publications Coordinator: Rebecca Skidmore

ISBN: 978-1-60378-125-1

Visit Hal Leonard Online at
www.halleonard.com

CONTENTS

The Day That Never Comes

Music by Metallica
Lyrics by James Hetfield

CELLO

Enter Sandman

Words and Music by
James Hetfield, Lars Ulrich and Kirk Hammett

CELLO

Fade to Black

Words and Music by
James Hetfield, Lars Ulrich,
Cliff Burton and Kirk Hammett

CELLO

Harvester of Sorrow

Words and Music by
James Hetfield and Lars Ulrich

CELLO

Slow Rock

Nothing Else Matters

Words and Music by
James Hetfield and Lars Ulrich

CELLO

One

Words and Music by
James Hetfield and Lars Ulrich

CELLO

Sad but True

Words and Music by
James Hetfield and Lars Ulrich

CELLO

Moderately slow

Seek & Destroy

Words and Music by
James Hetfield and Lars Ulrich

CELLO

The Thing That Should Not Be

Words and Music by
James Hetfield, Lars Ulrich and Kirk Hammett

CELLO

The Unforgiven

Words and Music by
James Hetfield, Lars Ulrich and Kirk Hammett

CELLO

Until It Sleeps

Words and Music by
James Hetfield and Lars Ulrich

CELLO

Welcome Home (Sanitarium)

Words and Music by
James Hetfield, Lars Ulrich and Kirk Hammett

CELLO

E-Z PLAY® TODAY SERIES

OVER 300 VOLUMES AVAILABLE!

The E-Z Play® Today songbook series is the shortest distance between beginning music and playing fun! Features of this series include:

- full-size books – large 9" x 12" format features easy-to-read, easy-to-play music

- accurate arrangements – simple enough for the beginner, but with authentic-sounding chords and melody lines

- minimum number of page turns

- thousands of songs – an incredible array of favorites, from classical and country to Christmas and contemporary hits

- lyrics – most arrangements include complete song lyrics

- most up-to-date registrations - books in the series contain a general registration guide, as well as individual song rhythm suggestions for today's electronic keyboards and organs

To see full descriptions of all the books in the series, visit:

HAL•LEONARD®

www.halleonard.com